HELPING
KIDS LIVE
THEIR FAITH

service projects that
make a difference

Mary Beth Jambor

ThomasMore®
– An RCL Company –

Allen, Texas

Send all inquiries to:
Thomas More
An RCL Company
200 East Bethany Drive
Allen, Texas 75002-3804

BOOKSTORES:
   Call Bookworld Companies 888-444-2524 or fax 941-753-9396
PARISHES AND SCHOOLS:
   Thomas More Publishing 800-822-6701 or fax 800-688-8356
INTERNATIONAL:
   Fax Thomas More Publishing 972-264-3719

Visit our website at **www.rclweb.com**

Printed in the United States of America

Library of Congress Number 99-75185

ISBN 0-88347-435-2

1 2 3 4 5   03 02 01 00 99

CONTENTS

INTRODUCTION

Helping *Kids Live Their Faith: Service Projects that Make a Difference* is written for you, the directors of religious education, youth ministers, catechists, teachers, volunteers, parents and all who are involved in the religious formation of children and youth. Each of you has an essential role in handing on faith to our young people. You provide them with the opportunities to both learn about and live out their faith. You also serve as a model of faith. You help them to see what it looks like to live a life of faith.

This book is organized in an easy-to-use format. The introduction explains the foundation on which the service project ideas are based and will help you understand how service is integral to the mission of the Church. It also offers suggestions for incorporating service into programs for children and youth.

Chapters 1 through 7 outline numerous service projects for young people of all ages. They are based on the seven themes of Catholic social teaching as outlined in 1998 by the United States Catholic Conference in Sharing Catholic Social Teaching: Challenges and Directions (1) Life and Dignity of the Human Person; (2) Call to Family, Community, and Participation; (3) Solidarity; (4) Option for the Poor and Vulnerable; (5) Dignity of Work and the Rights of Workers; (6) Rights and Responsibilities; and (7) Care of Creation.

Chapter 8 addresses peace. Unfortunately, we live in a society where some forms of violence are commonplace, and some become acceptable norms. Now, more than ever, we need to help young people recognize how violence and hatred can permeate our culture. Then, we need to give them the tools to live as peacemakers and the opportunity make a difference in the world.

Chapter 9 looks at fund-raising through the lens of our service mission. Here you will find creative fund-raising ideas that can simultaneously raise money for your youth service projects and provide a service to the parish or community.

Chapter 10 contains a list of "Dos and Don'ts." Whether you are a novice or experienced at organizing service projects with youth, take time to look at this chapter. It will help you avoid common mishaps and oversights.

This book concludes with a list of agencies, organizations, and offices. These can be valuable resources as you plan and prepare service projects.

SERVICE AND THE MISSION
OF THE CHURCH

The mission of the Church makes clear that service is integral to Catholics. The Church's mission is threefold. It includes word, worship, and service. We live out the mission of word by reading scripture and spreading the Good News of Jesus Christ. We carry out our mission of worship as we participate in liturgies and communal prayer. We live out the mission of service as we serve one another and the Church.

The Catholic Church has proclaimed its social teaching for more than one hundred years, beginning with Rerum Novarum in 1891. As recently as 1998, the United States Catholic

Conference published Sharing Catholic Social Teaching: Challenges and Directions. This document summarizes the history of Catholic social teaching. Seven social justice themes emerge and the bishops conclude by offering challenges and directions to parishes. Their goal is to encourage parishes to broaden, deepen, and strengthen Catholic social teaching in parish schools and formation programs.

Take time to teach young people about the mission of the Church and our long history of Catholic social teaching. As you do this, you will help them understand that service is not an extracurricular activity. At baptism, we are baptized into the common priesthood. And by virtue of our baptism, we are called to carry out the ministries of Jesus Christ in the world today. Service is essential to this call.

Before You Begin

As you begin to plan, develop, and implement service projects with young people, you will want to give adequate time and attention to your choices.

In choosing projects, keep in mind the ages of the children with whom you are working. Be sure that the project is developmentally appropriate for the group. Ask yourself if the children are physically, mentally, and socially capable.

Choose projects that work well with a group of young people. Serving in community with others is always beneficial. The old adage "many hands make the work lighter" holds true for a number of reasons.

1. A group can cut the time a large project may take.

2. Children may draw courage from their peers when they find themselves in unfamiliar settings.

3. Working together will help build community and friendships among the group.

Try to choose projects that vary in their circle of influence. For example, if one project serves the parish, perhaps the next project can serve people in another country. Help the children understand that they can serve people in their families, their parish, their neighborhoods, their communities, around their country, and other countries.

Be sure to take time to both prepare young people for a project and debrief afterward. Here are some simple suggestions:

Preparation

1. Tell the children about the people they will be serving.

2. Help the children see what the needs are of those they serve.

3. Provide an opportunity for the children to share what they hope for and what they may be concerned about.

4. Make your expectations clear. Include your behavior expectations.

5. Make the agency's expectations clear.

Debriefing

1. Ask the children what they learned about the people they served.

2. Ask the children what they learned about themselves.

3. Give the children the opportunity to talk about how they felt while they were doing the project. Were they nervous? Did they become more comfortable? Did they have a good time?

4. Ask the children to explain how they feel they made a difference in the lives of the people they served.

5. Ask the children to share what worked well.

6. Ask the children to share what did not work or what may have been frustrating. Give them a chance to share their suggestions.

7. If appropriate, provide an opportunity for the children to share stories of their service experience with their families and the parish community.

Finally, encourage the children to get involved. Help them to understand that each of us plays an essential role in our Church. We cannot stand around and point out to people what needs to or could be done. Help the young people see that if they don't do it, it won't get done!

CHAPTER 1

LIFE AND DIGNITY
OF THE HUMAN PERSON

As Catholics, we believe that each and every one of us is created in the image and likeness of God. Based on this belief, the Catholic Church asserts that all human life is sacred. Our belief in the sanctity of human life and the dignity of the human person provides the foundation of a moral vision of society. Upon this foundation, rests all Catholic social teaching.

In our society today, we may hear of some who promote a theory of "survival of the fittest."

Some use arguments about quality of life to support euthanasia and abortion as acts of mercy. As believers, we are called to reach out to the weak, the dying, the elderly, and the unborn with compassion. Abortion and euthanasia are not acts of mercy. Instead we believe our acts of mercy involve sharing Christ's love with those most in need.

"We believe that every person is precious, that people are more important than things, and that the measure of every institution is whether it threatens or enhances the life and dignity of the human person" (Sharing Catholic Social Teaching: Challenges and Directions #4).

Elderly

For many years, our parish has enjoyed a close relationship with our local nursing home where the staff always welcomes parish volunteers of all ages.

When I was in sixth grade, our catechist loved to sing. She taught us to sing some of the residents' favorite songs. During our visits, the residents filled the cafeteria and sang with us. Afterward, we would stroll through the hallways and share our music with those who were unable to come to the cafeteria.

Currently, our middle school youth group visits the care center on a regular schedule to play Bingo with the residents. The kids call the game, make certain the residents hear the numbers called, and distribute prizes. They also help any residents who need special assistance.

The residents look forward to spending time with the kids. After a little initial discomfort, the kids can see what a difference they make in the residents' lives. Our middle school youth enjoy Bingo at the care center so much that we have doubled our number of scheduled visits for the upcoming year!

1. **Build bird feeders and bird houses for seniors to hang in their yards. Find a church member who can teach young people how to make a bird house or feeder from a simple pattern. Explain the project to a local building supply store and request material donations.**

2. Make homemade treats for the homebound. This is a great project around the holidays. Thanks to the treats you make, these people will have treats to share with their holiday visitors. Deliver them personally or give them to volunteers who visit the homebound in your community. If you choose to send the treats with other volunteers, be sure to include a card.

3. Interview long-time members of your parish and put together a booklet of their stories and recollections. Make copies of the booklet and share it with the whole community.

4. Audio or video tape church services. Make copies of the tapes and give them to the homebound.

5. Take seniors grocery shopping or on other errands. This is an excellent ministry for high school youth!

6. Arrange to lead Bingo at a nursing home, senior center, or senior housing complex. Bring healthful treats or dimes for prizes. Be sure to speak loudly and clearly while calling the game. Have a few young people at each table to assist the players.

7. Arrange to visit a nursing home, senior center, or senior housing complex to play games with the residents. Games like cards, checkers, and chess provide a one-on-one opportunity to get to know the seniors.

8. Offer to assist the elderly in wrapping their Christmas gifts. Many seniors have difficulty with vision and arthritis which can make wrapping presents difficult.

9. Arrange to help seniors with holiday make-overs. Many seniors will have family visiting over the holidays and want to look their best. Volunteer to help them with fixing hair, trimming or polishing nails, and shaving.

10. Arrange to visit a senior facility to sing to and with the people. Learn some songs from when the seniors were young; they will love to sing them!

11. Bring flowers to an elderly person. You will let them know that they are special today and you may help them remember a time when a loved one brought them flowers. Ask them to share their memory with you.

12. Plant flowers and help tend the grounds of a senior facility. Residents who were once avid gardeners take great pleasure in enjoying such gardens.

13. Read and write letters for seniors. Failing vision and finger dexterity make reading and writing difficult for some elderly. Help them keep up with their correspondence.

14. Volunteer at a senior facility to help with their e-mail service. Many facilities provide computers for seniors to use, however they do not have enough staff to teach residents and program participants how to use the computers. Help seniors keep in touch with their friends and family by helping them learn about technology.

15. Host a "senior prom." Serve healthful treats and play music from your guests' era. Dance with those who can, and encourage everyone to move to the music. Be sure that hosts and hostesses dress well for this special occasion.

16. Host a holiday party. Decorate, serve treats, play games, and include music to celebrate any holiday. You might even like to help the seniors make a craft.

17. Provide meals-on-wheels to seniors on days that agencies do not provide them or volunteer with your local meals-on-wheels organization.

18. Offer rides to church for seniors who do not drive or those who choose not to drive in poor weather. Your parish priest or pastoral minister can identify people who are in need of transportation.

19. Invite a senior to sit with you at church. They may long for the days when they attended church with their spouse or family. For those newly widowed, attending Mass alone can be a difficult adjustment.

20. Make prayer cards or holiday cards for seniors. Deliver them to senior facilities or ask those who visit the homebound to deliver the cards.

21. Call nursing homes, care facilities, senior day-care centers, and senior centers to find out how you can help.

22. Adopt a grandparent. Seniors make excellent companions!

23. Become a prayer partner with a senior.

Expectant Parents and New Parents

1. Organize a diaper coupon collection. Distribute the coupons to parents in your church or donate them to a food shelf, or single parents.

2. Baby-sit for new parents. Even watching a baby for a short time at home so that a new mom can relax and take a bath or nap is helpful.

3. Host a baby shower for expectant parents in your church. Play games, bring gifts, and pray with the parents.

4. Create baby layettes or care packages for new parents. Include books, diapers, blankets, onesies, and other necessities. Distribute to single moms, food shelves, family shelters, area churches, or Catholic Charities Adoption Services.

5. Organize people to take turns providing meals for new parents during their first week at home with a new baby. Taking care of a new born is tiring and a tasty homemade meal is appreciated.

6. Pray for expectant parents and their unborn baby throughout the entire pregnancy. Send cards every few weeks to let the parents know you are still praying.

7. Organize a collection for Catholic Charities Adoption Services. Collection items could include: cribs, baby furniture, diapers, newborn clothing, blankets, baby formula.

8. Organize a maternity clothes collection. Make the clothing available to expectant moms in your parish or distribute them to your local Catholic Charities office. To locate the Catholic Charities office nearest you, contact their website at www.catholiccharitiesusa.org.

Mentally Challenged

About a dozen mentally handicapped adults live in the Northeast Residence, a group home in our community. For nearly twenty years, the Northeast Residence was housed in our vacated parish convent. A few years ago, the Northeast Residence purchased a large home nearby. The home is less institutional and better meets the needs of the residents and staff.

When the Northeast Residence changed locations, the parish Respect Life Committee very deliberately maintained our ties with the facility. During this time, our middle school youth began providing a Christmas party for the residents with assistance from the Respect Life Committee.

The Northeast Residence staff provides us with a list of names and gift ideas. The middle schoolers each donate $2. Then a couple of youth volunteers shop for the gifts. At the party, which is held at the facility, the Respect Life Committee serves treats and the middle schoolers distribute gifts to all the residents. And of course, we all sing Christmas carols together.

1. **Get involved with Special Olympics.** This organization utilizes both long-term and short-term volunteers. They need coaches to teach and train athletes. For the big events such as track meets, each athlete needs a host to guide them through the events of the day. Contact the Special Olympics website at www.specialolympics.org for more information.

2. **Set up a "special friends" buddy system for children in parish programs.** Mainstreaming children with special needs is the norm. However, we can further help these children

succeed if we pair them with another child
who will serve as both friend and advocate.

3. Develop a relationship with a group home
   in your community. Visit the facility on a
   regular basis to play games with residents,
   or host parties at the facility on special
   occasions.

4. Find out about camps or organizations in
   your area that serve the mentally challenged.
   Contact the facilities and discover how you
   can help. Facilities often provide training for
   volunteers who are willing to donate their
   time. Your diocese may have an office which
   specializes in ministry to those with special
   needs. They can be a resource for local
   agencies in need of volunteers.

5. Raise funds to send a mentally handicapped person in your community to a
   summer camp.

6. Set up a "special friends" buddy system for
   children who choose to participate in special
   youth events such as downhill skiing or
   visiting an amusement park. Be sure that
   parents of children of special needs know
   that "special friends" are available.

Physically Challenged

Our senior high youth group has made bathrooms accessible and has built wheelchair ramps. When modifying a bathroom, we must make certain we determine the needs. Does the resident want a nonskid floor and tub? Or does a wheelchair need to pass through the doorway? Sometimes "accessible" can mean safer, not necessarily wheelchair accessible.

Building a wheelchair ramp requires precision. We need to construct a ramp according to specifications which determine the percent grade of the incline and dimensions of corners. I find that high school youth have exceptional math skills and can easily figure out a plan for a ramp.

1. **Help with physical therapy. Those with severe physical disabilities need numerous hours of physical therapy everyday in their homes. Get involved with a team of volunteers and commit to helping with therapy sessions for an hour a week.**

2. Set up partners to host the physically challenged at church events. Be sure the hosts are aware of the location of accessible entrances and restrooms as well as any specific needs their partner may have.

3. Help those with poor vision with reading and writing. Paying bills and responding to mail can be made easier with a little assistance.

4. Offer to make phone calls for those who have difficulty hearing.

5. Make someone's home accessible. Build wheelchair ramps and install bathroom support rails.

6. If your church is not accessible to persons with disabilities, raise funds to make it accessible.

Terminally Ill

One of the largest events in our town each summer is the *Relay for Life*. The *Relay for Life* is a fundraiser for the American Cancer Society. Participants register in teams and team members find people to sponsor them. The teams commit to having at least one member walking a high-school track all night long.

Each year, the *Relay for Life* event in our community sells about 16,000 luminaries to honor cancer survivors or memorialize persons who have died of cancer. Our middle-schoolers help prepare luminaries all year long. Throughout the year, we fold bags and stamp them "In memory of _____" or "In honor of _____." On the day of the relay, youth groups around the area volunteer to place the bags around the track and fill them with a candle and sand.

This year, many members of our high-school youth group registered as a team and participated in the relay.

1. Visit someone who is in a hospice. Listen to their stories. Offer to read to them.

2. Become a prayer partner for someone who is terminally ill. Your pastor or pastoral minister can tell you who can benefit from your prayers.

3. Make cards for terminally ill patients with comforting messages. You might like to include scripture quotations.

4. Participate in fund-raisers for organizations that fund research and patient costs for terminal illnesses. For information contact local offices or websites of the following agencies: American Heart Association (www.amhrt.org), American Cancer Society (www.cancer.org), Cystic Fibrosis Foundation (www.cff.org), AIDS (www.worldaidsfoundation.org), Multiple Sclerosis (www.nmss.org), etc.

5. Contact a hospice in your area to find out about volunteers opportunities.

6. Organize a food specific drive for a hospice in your area. Hospices serve quite a bit of fresh fruit and juice. Support these organizations in their care for people who are dying.

Imprisoned

Our children make seasonal cards for prison inmates. However, we have learned that we must determine from prison staff what materials we can use to make the cards, since

some craft materials are not
allowed inside the prison.

Inmates do appreciate such
cards from children. We receive a
note a gratitude from the inmates
every time!

1. Organize a book collection for donations to the prison library.

2. Write letters and cards to inmates. Prison staff can make certain that children correspond only with inmates who are not a threat to the children.

3. Make Christmas stockings for inmates.

4. Spend time at a juvenile center and lead recreational activities. Juvenile center staff can help you know how to prepare.

5. Organize a toiletry collection for inmates or those moving to halfway houses. Because of the expense involved, prisons and halfway houses are often unable to provide them.

6. Call your local diocesan office of prison ministry to find out how you can get involved.

CHAPTER 2

CALL TO FAMILY, COMMUNITY, AND PARTICIPATION

We are called to live out our faith in our families and in our community. The opportunities for getting involved and making a difference in the lives of those around us are limitless!

While our society often promotes individualism, the Catholic Church teaches that we grow and achieve fulfillment in community (Sharing Catholic Social Teaching: Challenges and Directions, #5).

In the Church

1. Help with church mailings and other large, labor intensive projects. Folding, stuffing, labeling, and stamping a bulk mailing can be an overwhelming task for one person alone. Or it can become a time to visit and listen to music for a group. Catch up with friends and help the church at the same time!

2. Make publicity posters for parish events. Kids are often more creative and better with computers than many adults. Share creative talents and help publicize church events.

3. Get involved in liturgical ministries. Help kids understand that they do not necessarily have to be grownups to participate in these ministries. Encourage them to serve as readers, Eucharistic ministers, music ministers, altar servers, Children's Liturgy of the Word assistants, ministers of hospitality, or gift bearers.

4. As a youth group, take responsibility for all the hospitality ministries at Mass. Sign up to serve as greeters and ushers at one Mass a month. As children get older, they may prefer to serve with their peers rather than with their families.

5. Set up grade-level buddies. Pair a first-grade group with a fourth-grade group and assign each person a buddy. Throughout the year, bring the groups together for art projects, service projects, and celebrations. Young children thrive on special attention from older children. Older children feel good about themselves when they are helpful.

6. Organize prayer partners for children preparing for the sacraments. Make cards with the names of the children on them. Put them in a basket and place the basket near the entrance of the church. Invite parishioners to take a name and pray for the child throughout their preparation.

7. Create a prayer network. Provide a box where parishioners deposit their written prayer requests. On a regular basis, distribute a list of prayer requests to those who choose to serve the community through prayer. Your group of youngsters may even want to regularly pray in response to these prayer requests.

8. Make welcome cards for children and adults who are initiated into the church through Baptism and the RCIA (Rite of Christian Initiation of Adults). Arrange with the parish office to include the cards in the envelopes with the certificates.

9. Provide childcare at parish events. This service may make it possible for parents of young children to attend events.

10. Make luminaries for Christmas Eve Mass. Assemble the luminaries ahead of time. Then invite youth or families to take responsibility for setting up and cleaning up the luminaries before and after Mass.

11. Invite a friend or relative to a Mass or parish event. If you think your parish is wonderful, you can serve by helping someone else get connected to your community.

12. Offer to clean the church. Keeping the church tidy inside and out is a big job. Many hands can make the work quick and fun. Besides, the church belongs to us, the parish members. It is up to all of us to take care of our church.

13. Set up ministry mentors. Give kids an opportunity to find out more about a ministry before making a commitment. Ask volunteers to mentor young people who are interested in getting more involved. Kids can shadow volunteer ministers or find out what people find most rewarding about their ministry. This is a good activity for youngsters preparing for Confirmation.

14. Develop a plan for welcoming new parishioners to your church. The plan could include handing out welcome cards, inviting kids to youth events, or hosting a picnic where they can meet other parishioners.

15. Plan and host an all ages, alcohol-free New Year's Eve party. The party could include music, dancing, potluck dinner or desserts, games or raffles.

16. Invite a person who attends church alone to sit with you. Single adults, those newly divorced, or the elderly, may feel uncomfortable attending Mass alone. Invite someone to join you and your family.

17. Help families move. Let families know how much you will miss them and help them carry boxes and furniture.

In the Community

Each summer White Bear Lake, Minnesota area churches team up for *Summer Stretch*. *Summer Stretch* is an eight week summer program for middle-school youth. One day each week youth gather for a morning of service activities and an afternoon special event.

Over two-hundred young people participate each summer. This means more than twenty-five service sites benefit from our youth each week. And by the end of the summer, young people have experienced eight different service activities.

People who are out and about on Thursday mornings in White Bear Lake cannot help but notice all the kids in *Summer Stretch* t-shirts. The youth tend community gardens, help with summer maintenance projects in the local schools, provide activities for young children, and much more!

The youth ministers of the different churches appreciate the opportunity to minister as a team. We each take responsibility for a separate piece of the programming responsibilities. The kids enjoy participating with their friends as well as meeting new friends regardless of church affiliation.

1. Team up with other churches in your community for youth service projects. Young people will see how they can make a difference when all denominations work together. Be sure to provide time for socializing.

2. Paint murals over graffiti. Talk to city officials to get permission. Find out if a local hardware or paint store will provide the materials.

3. Host after-school activities for children. Help the children prepare puppet shows or design their own three ring circus. Also consider teaching crafts, reading books, and playing games and sports.

4. Welcome new students to school. Invite them to eat lunch with you and your friends. Also, help them find their way around the school and the community.

5. Volunteer at a local library. Libraries are always looking for people to read to children and shelve books.

6. Help with your community festival. A youth group can set up tables or chairs, post "no parking" signs, serve food, or take responsibility for cleanup. Talk to officials or

the Chamber of Commerce to find out how to get involved.

7. Bag groceries and help people to their cars at the grocery store. Parents with small children and seniors will welcome assistance. Grocery stores will also appreciate the opportunity to provide customers with extra hospitality.

8. Arrange to help with cleaning and grounds work at your school over the summer. Most schools save their biggest maintenance projects for the summer months. Young people can help move furniture, paint or repair playground equipment, or clean windows. Call the principal or the district maintenance and grounds office.

CHAPTER 3

SOLIDARITY

"Catholic social teaching proclaims that we are our brothers' and sisters' keepers, wherever they live. We are one human family, whatever our national, racial, ethnic, economic, and ideological differences" (Sharing Catholic Social Teaching: Challenges and Directions #5).

Solidarity means to "stand with." As Catholics, we believe that solidarity means "loving our neighbor," and we realize it is a global responsibility. As believers, we must not allow ourselves to slide into cultural norms and become indifferent or isolationist. We must keep ourselves informed and look for ways we can make a difference and "stand with" those in need.

Newly Arrived

A number of times each year,
I receive calls from people who have a
bed they no longer need. These
families prefer to donate their beds
rather than to sell them. In fact,
most families donate any bedding
they have along with the bed.

For families entering the country,
beds and bedding are expensive.
Many live for months or longer
sleeping on the floor.

Youth can pick up beds, bedding,
and sofa beds from families who
have donations and bring them to
agencies for distribution to families
in need.

1. Contact your local diocesan office of Immigration and Refugee Services to inquire about specific needs and how you can get involved.

2. Collect bedding and beds. Purchasing these items can be expensive. Bed or sofa bed donations can help a newly arrived family make a home, and blankets are always useful. School social workers or churches may know who can benefit from the donations.

3. Collect clothing for your climate. Often immigrants arrive with only the clothes they are wearing or clothing unsuited to the climate in their new home.

4. Provide transportation for immigrants. It may take months to get a driver's license. High-school age young people who drive can provide this essential service.

5. Teach a newly arrived family about the public transportation system in your community.

6. Offer to help with errands. Older youth or families can help a newly arrived family know where to go, how to get there, and whom to contact.

7. Offer hospitality and friendship. The most important gift we can share with immigrants is our love and care.

8. Donate religious gifts to immigrants. Catholic and Christian families will appreciate crucifixes, religious pictures, or rosaries for their homes.

9. Collect one-time-use cameras and photo albums. Distribute them to families so that they can take pictures of their children. You might like to collect donations to cover developing and printing costs as well.

10. Help newly arrived classmates at school. Offer to guide the new students to classes, through lunch, and to the administrative and counseling offices. If possible, invite them to join extracurricular activities.

11. Offer activities for migrant children. Youth can read books, tutor, teach crafts, organize sports and games, or lead religion classes.

Disaster Relief

On a regular basis, we place a glass bowl on a table near our baptismal font at church. In the bowl, we collect donations for a variety of causes, depending on current events.

We have collected for causes such
as flood relief and war refugees.
When the glass bowl appears,
people always look to read where their
donations will go.

1. Collect materials for disaster relief care packages. Care packages could include blankets, toiletries, clothing, and writing materials. Distribute the packages to Catholic Relief Services (www.catholicrelief.org) or the American Red Cross (www.redcross.org).

2. Flood relief can include making sand bags, shoveling mud out of homes, and cleaning homes and yards.

3. Walk on farm fields after a tornado or severe storm. The fields need to be searched for valuable items and cleared of debris. Form teams to walk the fields side-by-side.

4. Collect teddy bears for children displaced by fires, parental arrests, and natural disasters. Distribute the teddy bears to fire and police departments or to the American Red Cross. You can find your local American Red Cross Chapter through the American Red Cross website at www.redcross.org.

5. Organize a bottled water collection.

6. Anytime disaster happens, provide a basket in the common areas of the church for donations. Eventually, members of your parish will develop a habit of checking for the basket each time they come for Mass. Be sure to place a sign near the basket that describes where the funds will be sent.

7. Host a shower for a family who lost their home in a fire. Invite parish members to give kitchen utensils, clothing, toiletries, towels, and blankets as gifts.

8. If you can collect a large volume of supplies for disaster relief, transportation businesses may be willing to deliver the donations for free. Contact airlines or trucking companies who could help. Also, check with your local National Guard who may be available to deliver the donations.

Missions and Poverty Abroad

1. Collect donations for Oxfam International. Oxfam is dedicated to fighting poverty and injustice around the world. To find out more about Oxfam International, contact their website at www.oxfam.org.

2. Collect donations for Catholic Relief Services. Catholic Relief Services is active in over eighty countries responding to both long-term and immediate needs of people in poverty. To find out more about Catholic Relief Services, contact their website at www.catholicrelief.com.

3. Sponsor a child through an agency that provides children with food and education. Be sure that you choose an organization that will be most effective.

4. Donate livestock. Heifer Project International (HPI) invites people to purchase farm animals for families living in poor countries. To find out more about HPI contact their website at www.heifer.org.

5. Be a pen-pal with a missionary kid. Many missionaries are living in other countries with their entire family. Missionary kids would welcome the opportunity to correspond with someone their own age from their home country.

CHAPTER 4

OPTION FOR THE POOR AND VULNERABLE

Since the Second Vatican Council, the Catholic Church has established that the needs of the poor must come first. In Matthew 25:31–46, Jesus instructs us on how to care for the poor and vulnerable:

"For I was hungry and you gave me food, I was thirsty and you gave me drink, a stranger and you welcomed me, naked and you clothed me, ill and you cared for me, in prison and you visited me."

General

We have two collections that our parish welcomes year after year. One is a shoe collection. Anytime children outgrow their shoes, they can bring their shoes to the parish office.

About once a month, volunteers bring the shoes to local shelters. Many children outgrow their shoes before they wear out. Both parents and kids welcome the opportunity to donate their shoes rather than throw them away.

Families also look forward to our after-Christmas winter clothing drive. By January, families know what winter clothes no longer fit their children. Also, Christmas has come and gone. New jackets and sweaters may take the place of clothing that can now be donated.

1. Arrange to serve a meal at a soup kitchen or shelter. Some shelters provide the food for you to prepare and serve, while other shelters may ask you to furnish the food. Check with the shelter to find out their volunteer

requirements, such as age, adult/child ratio, attire, and food preparation regulations.

2. Arrange to visit a shelter. If possible, talk to guests, listen to their stories, and offer to play cards. Staff at the shelter can offer tips on preparing for the visit and interacting with guests.

3. Organize a food collection. Contact the local food shelf to find out if there are particular food items they need. You might like to do a specific food drive.

4. Organize a coat and mitten collection. Fall and after Christmas are good times to hold these drives. Many children outgrow their winter clothes each year or replace them at Christmas time. Attach mittens and gloves to keep pairs together.

5. Organize clothing collections as the seasons change. These are the times of year that people go through their closets. You will make donating easier for people while providing donations for those in need.

6. Organize a shoe and sock collection. People on the street suffer severely from foot problems. It is nearly impossible for the homeless to keep their feet clean and dry.

Shelters often provide foot baths. However, clean socks and shoes are always in demand.

7. Arrange to work at a food shelf. Donations need to be gathered from area drop boxes and organized at the agency. Food also needs to be parceled for distribution.

8. Volunteer at a food bank. Second Harvest is a national food bank network. Each food bank needs volunteers to divide huge quantities of food into smaller portions to be given to those in need. Once food is divided, a variety of foods needs to be packaged for people to pick up. To find the Second Harvest nearest you call 1-800-532-FOOD or contact their website at www.secondharvest.org.

9. Make homemade desserts for shelters that offer free meals. Call the Catholic Charities office in your diocese or contact the Catholic Charities USA website at www.catholiccharitiesusa.org to locate shelters in your area.

10. Make quilts and pillows for the homeless. Distribute them to shelters in your area.

11. Purchase food with all the trimmings for a holiday meal. Bring your donation to

Church or to the local food shelf. Holiday meals can be costly, and low-income families will appreciate your generosity.

12. Organize a collection of discarded lawn mowers or cars. Repair and donate them. High-school autotech classes or technical schools may be willing to assist with or complete repairs.

13. Organize an all-night-sleep-out to raise homelessness awareness in your community. Talk to city officials to arrange permission for the sleep-out to take place in a park or public space. Remember, sleeping bags and tents are not allowed. Only cardboard boxes are permitted. Post informational flyers throughout the area inviting people to visit your temporary homeless community.

Children in Poverty

Young children love to celebrate their birthdays! In our parish, we provide children with the opportunity to help children in poverty celebrate their birthdays. All year round, we collect cake mixes, frosting, candles, and small toys. As supplies accumulate, we assemble birthday boxes. Volunteers deliver

the boxes to local food shelves and
shelters. Our kids feel good about
themselves when they realize they
can help other children feel special
on their birthdays.

1. Organize a children's book collection. Donate
   the books to shelters, food shelves, or
   churches and schools in low-income areas.

2. Collect used and new bikes and toys. Don't
   forget outdoor toys like balls and jump ropes.
   If necessary repair them and donate them.
   Bring the donations to shelters, food shelves,
   or churches in low-income areas.

3. Collect new and used school supplies. The
   end of the school year is a great time for this
   collection. As children pack up their lockers
   and desks, invite them to donate the unused
   portion of notebooks, makers, crayons,
   colored pencils, pencils, and pens. Or, as
   children prepare for a new school year, invite
   them to purchase items to donate. Bring or
   send the donations to schools and churches
   in low-income areas.

4. Make special treats for children at food
   shelves or shelters. Make candy treat bags or
   decorate cookies and cupcakes. These kinds
   of treats are a rare contribution for children
   in poverty. The treats will be appreciated

and will help the children know that others care for them.

5. Organize a collection and make baby kits for shelters. Collect items for baby care-packages. Items could include formula, diapers, washcloths, baby bath soap, and wipes. Distribute the care-packages to shelters and food shelves.

6. Make Birthday Boxes. Help children in poverty celebrate their birthdays. Collect cake mixes, frosting, candles, and small toys. Decorate bakery cake boxes and fill with birthday items. Be sure that toys are appropriate for both boys and girls. Also, keep all ages of children in mind. Distribute the Birthday Boxes to shelters and food shelves.

7. Collect inexpensive kids games and toys for shelters. Ideas might include decks of cards, crayons, bubbles, balls, jacks, jump ropes, coloring books, and books. Distribute to shelters and transitional housing facilities.

8. Organize an "adopt a family" program at Christmas. Find out the ages, sizes, and needs of families in need and give them to people who will be providing the gifts. If you do not have donors wrap presents, you might like to ask donors to donate gift wrap paper.

Most families in need will want to remain anonymous. Be sure to respect their confidentiality. Parish staff, food shelves, and shelters may be able to provide possible recipients.

9. Make toys for children. Invite those with the skills to teach your youth group how to make a few toys. You may be able to find donations for materials. Distribute the toys to shelters, food shelves, and low-income churches.

10. Arrange to host a picnic or a party for children living in a shelter or transitional housing facility. Plan games and activities. Provide and serve special treats.

CHAPTER 5

DIGNITY OF WORK
AND THE RIGHTS OF WORKERS

"Work is more than a way to make a living; it is a form of continuing participation in God's creation. If the dignity of work is to be protected, then basic rights of workers must be respected. Respecting these rights promotes an economy that protects human life, defends human rights, and advances the well-being of all" (Sharing Catholic Social Teaching: Challenges and Directions, #5).

As Catholic consumers, we are called to inform ourselves about the working conditions of people who make the products we purchase. We must also treat all people in service careers with respect.

> During the Gulf War, many of our parishioners had friends and family who were sent to the Persian Gulf. For a few weeks, we placed a note in the parish bulletin letting people know that if they had loved ones in the Gulf, we would send cards to them. Quickly, the addresses poured in. We told the children a little bit about each person and provided them with materials for making cards.
>
> Every person who received cards wrote back to us. They told about life in the Persian Gulf and how they missed home and their families. Some sent pictures of the planes they flew and the tents where they lived. One man even came to visit the children after the war.

Most high school students have more disposable income than any

58

other age group. Also during these years, young people are developing a social conscience. This is a perfect time to invite kids to investigate what types of labor conditions and businesses they support with their dollars.

Our young people discovered that from clothing to soccer balls, manufacturers utilize child labor camps in third-world countries. Once they informed each other about their findings, they committed to patronizing only businesses who followed particular labor regulations.

1. Distribute a list of retailers who are committed to following just labor regulations. Call your local Catholic Charities Office of Social Justice or contact the Catholic Charities website at www.catholiccharitiesusa.org for a list. The U.S. Department of Labor website at www.dol.gov is another resource.

2. Arrange to host a teacher appreciation breakfast or cookies and cider for teachers after school.

3. Order pizzas for the school custodians to enjoy while you take responsibility for the cafeteria setup and cleanup for a day.

4. Arrange to serve hot chocolate to school bus drivers as they drop off students at school. If possible, serve them on a cold winter morning.

5. Leave treats for your mail carrier in the mailbox. If you live in a warm climate, a bottle of water would make an appropriate treat.

6. When a person in a service position is exceptional, let his/her boss know!

7. Offer to help teachers, church staff, and others with projects.

8. Write letters to military personnel who are away from their families. Put a note in the parish bulletin requesting names and addresses of those who would appreciate a letter.

9. Bring flowers to the school secretary to have on her desk. School secretaries need to be near their desks all day. Flowers will let her know how much you appreciate her.

10. Make thank-you cards for the pastor. Try
    to thank the pastor for something specific.
    You might even consider using scripture
    quotations on the cards.

CHAPTER 6

RIGHTS AND
RESPONSIBILITIES

"The Catholic tradition teaches that human dignity can be protected and a healthy community can be achieved only if human rights are protected and responsibilities are met. . . . Corresponding to these rights are duties and responsibilities—to one another, to our families, and to the larger society" (Sharing Catholic Social Teaching: Challenges and Directions, #5).

As Catholics, we are called to act in order to ensure that the rights of all people are protected.

Begin by naming those who suffer from injustice. Then consider how to act.

Youth in our parish offer a 'Random Acts of Kindness Day' each spring. We help elderly parishioners and community members with all sorts of spring cleanup chores. We trim shrubs, rake leaves, prepare gardens, and spread mulch. We also stain decks, wash windows, and move furniture from storage onto patios.

To find people who need assistance, our pastor and parish nurse provide us with a list of people to contact. We also call people who have lost a spouse in the last year. To make certain that we don't miss anyone, we also advertise our free service in the parish bulletin.

Each year, participation has grown. The first year we helped a dozen residents. This year, more than fifty volunteers helped nearly thirty residents!

We divide into work crews of about five: four youth and one adult. The adults provide transportation and assure the participants' safety.

Each crew works at two or sometimes three homes.

Residents enjoy our company as much as they appreciate our hard work. Some call me in advance to find out what kind of soda or snacks the kids like. Others send thank-you cards and pictures afterward. The kids enjoy hearing the residents' stories about how our town or church used to be.

At the end of the day, we gather for dinner and share stories about our experiences.

———

High-school youth in our parish have participated in Workcamp for the past six years. For many young people Workcamp is a formative and life-changing experience.

Workcamp is an ecumenical youth camp organized through Group Publishing. Every summer, Group offers about thirty camps around the country. Each camp involves 300–400 youth and youth leaders.

Through Workcamp, we spend a week repairing, painting, and weatherizing homes for people trapped in poverty. Home repair projects include: siding, roofing, replacing windows or doors, replacing stairs, and painting.

The primary goal of Workcamp is to help young people grow n their faith while they serve. By the end of the week, kids know that they can make a difference!

———

Our middle-school and high-school youth thoroughly enjoy playing with younger children. During the summer, we organize activities for children living in a local family violence shelter. At first our middle-school youth didn't understand what a shelter was or how children happened to be there. If you bring your youth to volunteer at a shelter help them to understand that a shelter provides safety for people who have nowhere else to go.

1. Arrange a youth mission trip. Plan to spend a week away from home helping residents trapped in poverty. Projects could include painting, replacing doors and windows, roofing, and repairing foundations. Group Workcamps offers summer mission experiences for church youth groups. For more information call 1-800-774-3838 or contact their website at www.groupworkcamps.com.

2. Get involved with Habitat for Humanity. For more information about Habitat for Humanity call the office in your area or contact their website at www.habitat.org.

3. Organize a "Random Acts of Kindness" day. Offer to help older parishioners with yard cleanup in the spring and fall. Although most seniors are able to live independently, raking and trimming bushes can be too difficult. Advertise your free labor in the parish bulletin. In addition, your pastor or pastoral minister can help identify people in need. Also, be sure to contact those who are recently widowed.

4. Participate in an Urban Immersion Retreat. Plan to spend some time learning about various urban issues as well as serving in agencies, such as shelters or low-income childcare centers. Contact your diocesan office of Social Justice or an urban parish for ideas and planning assistance.

5. Organize a paint-a-thon. Spend a weekend painting a home for someone in need. Ask local hardware and paint stores to donate materials. Your pastor or pastoral minister can identify those who could benefit from this project.

6. Host a speaker on the issue of homosexuality. Ask the speaker to be sure to explain how many homosexuals suffer from prejudice.

7. Organize or host a blood drive. The American Red Cross will come to your facility and utilize your volunteers. People are needed for tasks such as typing and serving juice and cookies. For more information, contact the American Red Cross and www.redcross.org.

8. Arrange to plant flower or vegetable gardens with low-income families. Ask a local nursery to donate supplies or provide supplies at a discounted price.

9. Set up a mentorship program in your parish. Pair older children with younger children who can benefit from some special attention. A commitment of about three hours a month is appropriate. Mentors can help young children with homework or invite young children to community events.

10. Collect items for transitional housing care packages. Items could include toiletries, bedding, clothing, notebooks and pens. Call your diocesan office to locate a transitional housing facility in your area.

11. Contact a church community that has a different ethnic background than your parish. Arrange to do a service project involving youth from both communities. Your diocesan youth ministry office may be able to help you locate another parish.

12. Arrange to build playground equipment in a low-income neighborhood or daycare. Contact churches or schools in low-income areas to find out where you can help.

13. Offer to weatherize homes. Spend a day repairing windows and screens, caulking, and painting homes for people in need. Ask a local hardware store to donate materials for the project. Your pastor or pastoral minister can help identify those who can benefit from this project.

14. Organize a low-cost or free baby-sitting service for single parents who are in school. Advertise the service in the parish bulletin, at local high schools, technical schools, community colleges, and colleges.

15. Host kids' activities at a shelter. Plan a few hours of organized games, crafts, treats, and other festivities at a family shelter. Contact your local diocesan office to locate a shelter in your area.

16. Collect multicultural toys, books, and dolls to donate to a childcare center.

17. Develop a drama team to do a presentation on racism and other forms of prejudice. Offer to present the drama to other churches in your community.

18. Collect religious pictures and sacramentals to send to third-world countries. All of the religious art and books in the eastern block countries were destroyed during the reign of communism. Now these countries welcome religious gift donations. Contact your diocesan office to find out where to send your donations.

19. Your diocese may have a missionary affiliation. Call your diocesan office to find out how youth can support the diocesan missionary effort.

20. Missions are not always in other countries. Contact your diocesan office to find out how to help the missionary dioceses in the United States.

CHAPTER 7

CARE FOR CREATION

"The Catholic tradition insists that we show our respect for the Creator by our stewardship of creation. Care for the earth . . . is a requirement of our faith" (Sharing Catholic Social Teaching: Challenges and Directions, #6).

Opportunities for caring for creation are as abundant and various as God's creations themselves. Whether you are looking for a large or small, local or global, long-term or short-term project, you can find a stewardship project to suit your group.

Our local school district adopted a section of highway. Since school is not in session throughout the summer, area youth groups pitch in and take care of the highway for a few months.

———

Our local nature center offers a variety of volunteer opportunities for youth. Sometimes we replenish the supply of wood chips on the trails and pick up litter. Other times we plant trees or help with groups of small children.

———

Our youth help tend gardens in the city parks. When we work together, we can quickly weed a large area. We enjoy chatting while we work. Time flies and suddenly gardening is no longer a back breaking chore.

1. Arrange to spend a weekend at a co-op or organic farm. Plan to help with chores as well as take time to learn about the environmental benefits of co-op and organic farming.

2. Encourage car pools for church youth activities. If your parish is large, set up a

carpool database to facilitate carpooling in neighborhoods. Invite young people to keep track of the results of the carpools, such as gallons of gas saved and the effect on the environment. Print the results in the parish newsletter.

3. Research and write articles for the Church newsletter about how to protect the environment. Be sure to find out article deadlines and space availability well in advance.

4. Arrange to plant bulbs or flowers at Church, at school, at a cemetery, or elsewhere in the community. Ask a local nursery to donate plants or provide them at a reduced cost. Be sure to maintain the flowers throughout the season.

5. Arrange to plant trees. Schools, parks, churches, and other nonprofit organizations could benefit from this project.

6. Organize a recycling program in your parish. Provide containers and label them. Also be sure to arrange regular collection times.

7. Pick up litter at area parks, schools, playgrounds, and other public areas.

8. Offer a pet-care class at Church for young children. Older children can share their

expertise. You might consider inviting a veterinarian or Humane Society volunteer to lead the class.

9. Arrange to host a "blessing of the animals" event in your parish. Invite people of all ages to bring their pets to be blessed on the feast of St. Francis of Assisi on October 4.

10. Offer to play with a pet in your neighborhood. Pets need exercise and attention to thrive. Find out if there is a pet in your neighborhood who could benefit from a walk or some extra attention.

11. Offer to help with animal migration. As we develop more and more of our land and pollute our waters, we can inhibit animal migratory patterns. Get involved with an agency that helps and protects these animals.

12. Garden for a neighbor. Plant and care for a flower garden for an elderly or single-parent neighbor. Your kindness will bring cheer to them everyday!

13. Organize a Christmas tree recycling program. Contact your local recycling center for information.

14. Hold a fund-raiser in order to donate trash cans or recycling containers to parks and

schools. Contact your local parks department or school principal to inquire about their needs.

15. Plant and tend flower gardens at a nursing home. The residents will enjoy the flowers when they sit outside.

16. Offer to help at a nature center. Most nature centers rely on volunteers to greet guests, maintain trails, and keep grounds clean.

17. Volunteer at a wildlife refuge. Learn about animals while you work to protect them.

18. The Humane Society is another organization that relies heavily on volunteers. For more information contact the Humane Society website at www.nhes.org.

19. Participate in Earth Day. Earth Day is a national day set aside for cleaning up and caring for our creation. Choose Earth Day, April 24, to carry out stewardship projects.

20. Adopt a highway. Take responsibility for maintaining a section of highway in your community. For more information contact your State Department of Transportation.

21. Adopt a rainforest. One way we can save the rainforests is to purchase rainforest lands an acre at a time. To learn more about the rainforest or to purchase an acre contact The Nature Conservancy website at www.tnc.org.

22. Take responsibility for keeping a section of a river clean. Ask local disposal companies to remove the trash you collect for free. For more information on saving our rivers contact American Rivers at www.amrivers.org.

23. Adopt a whale. You will receive the name and a picture of your whale immediately. As your whale is sighted over the years, you will receive updates. For more information contact the Pacific Whale Foundation website at www.pacificwhale.org.

CHAPTER 8

PEACE

Bringing peace was essential to Jesus' ministry on earth. As Catholics, we are called to continue his peacemaking ministry. We must take a firm stand against violence and hatred in our world.

"Blessed are the peacemakers, for they shall be called children of God." Matthew 5:9

A Peace Pole is an international symbol of peace. It is a six-sided wooden post. On each side Plexiglas plaques display the phrase, "May Peace Prevail On Earth" in twelve different languages.

Our youth group raised funds to purchase a Peace Pole. We planted it in the center of our church yard and surrounded it with a small flower garden. We dedicated our Peace Pole in memory of a parishioner who served our parish for many years as an advocate for youth.

1. Organize activities for children at a family violence shelter. Activities could include tutoring, crafts, games, sports, or reading books. To locate a shelter near you, call your diocesan office or Catholic Charities.

2. Write, sign, and commit to keeping a peace pledge. Brainstorm ways in which you can live peacemaking lives. Put the ideas into the form of a pledge. Invite all members of the group to sign and commit to keeping the pledge. Post the pledge and invite all parish members to join the youth in living as peacemakers.

3. Organize a neighborhood block party. Invite all the neighbors to gather outside for an evening to get to know one another. Lead games for the children. Consider taking pictures of each household and making a neighborhood directory.

4. Set up a peer mediation program. Train youth as peer mediators. Be sure to utilize the peer mediators for conflict resolution with their peers at parish programs. For information on peer mediation training materials, talk to a school counseling office or contact the Augsburg Fortress Publishers website at www.augsburgfortress.org.

5. Invite young people to research and write articles about violence-related issues for the church newsletter. Topics might include guns, music, movies, video games, pornography, abortion, crime, and drug and alcohol abuse.

6. Participate in war relief efforts. Contact the Catholic Relief Services website at www.catholicrelief.org or the American Red Cross website at www.redcross.org for more information.

7. Raise funds for and plant a Peace Pole as a reminder to your community to live as peacemakers. For more information on the Peace Pole Network, contact The Peace Pole Makers USA, 3534 Lanham Road, Maple City, Michigan 49664. Or call (616) 334-4567.

CHAPTER 9

FUND-RAISING

Occasionally you may need to raise money to fund your service projects. This chapter describes a number of fund-raising ideas which also provide a service to the parish and community.

Our high-school youth sponsor two parties a year for middle-schoolers to raise money for the summer mission trip. In the fall, we host a dance and haunted house. Each high-school kid takes responsibility

for a specific piece of the event.
Some are DJs, others make scary
scenes inside the haunted house,
and some run the snackbar. The
middle-schoolers liked the haunted
house so much that many paid to go
through it two or three times!

In the spring, we host a dance
and an indoor eighteen-hole
miniature golf course. Pairs of high-
schoolers design golf holes, and each
hole has a theme. Themes included:
sports, the '50s, Hawaii, and Barbie.
Learn from our experience and try
not to make the holes too difficult.
The middle-schoolers like the holes
they can play in 4–5 shots with the
best scenery.

1. Hold a car wash. Instead of charging a fixed
   price, ask for donations.

2. Organize a garage sale. Invite the entire
   parish to donate items for the sale. You will
   be raising money while you provide people
   with an opportunity to purchase items at a
   lesser cost.

3. Host a pancake breakfast on a Sunday
   morning. You will be helping to build

community in your parish while you raise money for a worthwhile cause.

4. Host a spaghetti dinner. Almost everybody likes spaghetti, and it is easy to make for large groups of people.

5. Host a Valentine dinner. Consider offering childcare or activities for children so that parents can have a chance to sit and talk with each other.

6. Host a Friday night fish fry during Lent.

7. Sell poinsettias for Christmas and Easter lilies for Easter. This fund-raiser provides people with an opportunity to support the youth and a convenient way to purchase their holiday plant at Church.

8. Hold a bake sale after Mass. Ask youth to bake. In addition, invite all parishioners to donate goodies for the sale. Homemade items are a special treat. Consider scheduling the bake sale near a holiday like Valentine's Day or Mothers' Day and decorate treats for the occasion.

9. Team up with area chefs to plan and host a spectacular dinner. The chefs can help the young people choose a menu and teach them how to prepare and serve the meal. The dinner builds community, raises funds for

youth programs, and gives chefs an opportunity to introduce young people to culinary arts.

10. Arrange to work a concession booth. Many professional teams' stadiums utilize non-profit volunteers in their food services. The organization that the volunteers represent is paid for each volunteer. Call your local stadium for more information.

11. Arrange to bag and carry groceries. Many grocers are willing to pay for extra help during busy times of the year, such as before Thanksgiving and Christmas. You will make a hectic time of the year better for the store and its customers while earning money for youth projects.

12. Organize and advertise a "hire a hand" program in your parish. Many parishioners are willing to pay for a little extra help around their homes and yards. This service can supply those looking for help with hard-working, reliable assistance.

13. If you can, find a donor who will match contributions up to a certain amount. Matching contributions may encourage more people to donate since their contribution will be doubled.

14. Provide sponsorship opportunities. Sometimes people prefer to donate money rather than purchase an item or service. Give people a vehicle for making financial contributions to youth participants.

15. Publish a list of materials that you need. For example, you may need painting supplies and caulking guns for a mission trip. Both businesses and individuals may donate what you need. Remember that people will not know what you need unless you ask.

16. When you near the end of a fund drive, publish the amount you still need to reach your goal. The information may encourage people who have been thinking about donating to act.

17. Sell religious gifts. Bring a vendor to your parish to sell crosses, books, and other religious gift items. Arrange for a percentage of the sales to go to fund your service project. A good time of year for this sale is shortly before First Communion or Confirmation.

18. Sponsor an evening at a fast food restaurant. Some fast food restaurants will specify an evening for a nonprofit

organization. A portion of the sales will go to the organization. All you need to do is encourage people to eat at that restaurant on your specific night.

19. Have high-school youth host special events for junior-high or middle-school youth. Possible events might include dances, a haunted house, or an indoor mini-golf course.

20. Organize kids' carnival games at a community or parish festival. These games are simple and can be staffed by children of all ages.

CHAPTER 10

DOS AND DON'TS

* Do plan time for preparation before and debrief afterward.

* [Do] Be aware of confidentiality. You need to protect both the children and the people you serve.

* Do involve young people in the decision-making process as you choose service projects.

* Do take time to visit with those you serve. Some people, especially the elderly, may be lonely and appreciate the company.

* Do offer the same opportunities to both boys and girls. Don't discriminate.

* Do make both your own and the agency's expectations clear.

* Do follow all agency guidelines regarding adult to child ratios, attire restrictions, age restrictions, and behavior expectations.

* Do give good directions to the facility. Don't waste time lost in traffic.

* [Do] Be sure that all volunteers will be utilized. Don't have some kids simply watching while others are busy serving.

* [Do] Be sure that the purpose of the project is well-defined. Discuss with young people the effect the ministry will have on those they serve.

* Do help young people recognize that when they serve, they also receive.

* Do discourage unnecessary complaints. Both positive and negative attitudes are contagious. Help kids understand that it is a privilege to have an opportunity to share their gifts with others.

* Do discourage youth from judging those they serve. Compassion involves putting ourselves in someone else's place and understanding

their circumstances. We are called to serve with compassion, not judge.

* Do support and empower young people as they learn to serve and expand their comfort zone.

* Don't make service a requirement to be completed outside of program time. Instead, integrate service into the program so that young people can learn about the importance of service. Then, invite and inspire young people to get more involved in living their life of faith in service to others.

* Do avoid projects that are simply "busy work" with no real effect.

* Do provide an opportunity for young people to share their service-project experience with their families and the parish community. Culminate a project with a potluck supper, slides, and a chance for young people to share their stories.

* Don't allow people to take advantage of young people. Don't let your youth get involved in a project that is so horrendous no one else would do it.

* Do find people with the skills and gifts you need and utilize them in the program. For example you may need people to teach youth

about the elderly or how to repair a window. You may need drivers and cooks. Remember, the adults who assist you with service projects provide a powerful example to the young volunteers. The more opportunities you provide, the more people of faith the youngsters will come to know.

* Do provide every opportunity you can to invite and allow all parishioners to support young people and their service projects.

Agencies, Organizations, and Offices

1. Every diocese has a Catholic Charities office. To find the office in your area contact the Catholic Charities website at www.catholiccharitiesusa.org.

2. Catholic Relief Services provides disaster relief and assistance to refugees. For more information, contact the Catholic Relief Services website at www.catholicrelief.org.

3. The American Red Cross provides disaster relief, and assistance to war refugees. The American Red Cross also organizes blood, organ, bone marrow, and tissue donations. For more information, contact the American Red Cross website at www.redcross.org.

4. Call your local school principal or school district office to find opportunities for service.

5. Call city offices to find out how to get youth involved in community service experiences. Your community may need assistance with parks, beaches, festivals, landscaping, and gardening.

6. Call county offices for information about service opportunities for youth. The county may need assistance with parks, beaches, special events, landscaping, and gardening.

91

7. The local community counseling center will be aware of agencies in your area where you can serve, such as shelters and transitional housing.

8. Call the volunteer coordinator at local nursing homes and care facilities to offer your services.

9. Special Olympics offers athletic training and competition for mentally challenged children and adults. For more information contact the Special Olympics website at www.specialolympics.org.

10. The Salvation Army is a Christian organization committed to a variety of social justice programs. For more information contact the Salvation Army website at www.salvationarmy.org.

11. Second Harvest is the largest food bank network in the United States. For more information contact the Second Harvest website at www.secondharvest.org.

12. Oxfam International is committed to addressing the issues of poverty and hunger. The organization is currently active in over 100 countries around the world. For more information, contact the Oxfam International website at www.oxfam.org.

13. Heifer Project International invites donors to contribute toward the purchase of farm animals for families in poverty. Through this program the Heifer Project works to help families achieve a sustainable source of income and food. For more information contact the Heifer Project International website at www.heifer.org.

14. The U.S. Department of Labor has an active role in ensuring just working conditions. For more information contact the U.S. Department of Labor NO SWEAT website www.dol.gov.

15. Group Workcamps offers summer mission trip experiences around the country for church youth groups. For more information call 1-800-774-3838 or contact their website at www.groupworkcamps.com.

16. Habitat for Humanity is a Christian organization committed to providing housing for low-income families. For more information contact the Habitat for Humanity website at www.habitat.org.